THE THERAPY GROUP
and other poems

Gillian Hutchinson

First published in 2020 by Hawkes Design and Publishing Limited
Design by Amanda Carroll

Text and photographs © Gillian Hutchinson 2020.

All rights reserved. No part of this publication may be reproduced, stored in a retrieval system or transmitted in any form or by any means, electronic, mechanical, photocopying and recording or otherwise, without permission in writing by the publisher. Gillian Hutchinson has asserted her moral right to be identified as the author of this work.
ISBN 978-1-9998335-9-6

CONTENTS

INTRODUCTION
5

THE THERAPY GROUP
7

SEASONS
29

IN SOMBRE MOOD
41

IDLE THOUGHTS
55

FAMILY
73

Tate People

INTRODUCTION

I rarely set out to write a poem. The ideas usually come to me when I am thinking about an experience or emotional reaction and the first two lines come into my mind.

This is especially true of the poems in The Therapy Group. I attended this group after a period when I had been feeling unwell for some time and my GP, who could not find a cause, suggested I was depressed and should see a psychotherapist. I had seen a Reflexologist who told me there was something wrong but she could not be specific, so I agreed to go to the group feeling it would be interesting. I found it fascinating, but left the group when I changed my job and it was no longer convenient. Some time later a long awaited scan revealed that I had an advanced tumour. That was over twenty years ago.

The poems in The Therapy Group were written during the time the group was meeting. They reflect my ideas of what was going on which may not, of course, be accurate. They were all written at the time and I have kept them in the order in which they were written. The names have been changed.

The rest of the poems have been written over many years up to the present day, and I have now decided to put them together with some of my favourite photographs.

Gillian Hutchinson

In Reflective Mood

THE THERAPY GROUP

FIRST MEETING	*Page 8*
AFTER THE NOVELTY	*9*
THE GROUP	*10*
MARY	*11*
BETH	*12*
POWER	*13*
NICHOLAS	*15*
THOMAS	*16*
MAY	*17*
GILLIAN	*18*
ROBERT	*19*
STEPHEN	*20*
SILENCE	*21*
GILLIAN 2	*22*
FRUSTRATION	*23*
MARIONETTES	*24*
ENVOI	*25*
AND NEVER HAVE TO SAY GOODBYE	*26*
UNTITLED	*27*

FIRST MEETING

Silence
                stretches
                              uneasily.

The occupants of the room
Shift in their seats
And do not meet
Each others' eyes.

Someone coughs.

The leader
                waits
                              impassively.

The tension strains. A nerve
Abruptly breaks.
Someone speaks
And everyone else
Sighs
In relief.

AFTER THE NOVELTY

After the novelty – boredom.
I've heard them before,
The problems and personal worries.
What's it all for,
This constant preoccupation
With husbands and wives
And families and friends and relations?
Will all our lives
Be changed by perpetual discussion
Of fathers and mothers
Of siblings and schooldays and workmates?
I look at the others –
Some talking too much and some silent,
frightened to speak,
And question the wisdom and value
Of coming each week.

I know what is going to happen,
Tom will be late
Interrupting the ritual discussion
Of jobs the men hate.
Beth will start crying as usual
To show how she feels
About all those terrible traumas
She never reveals.
Mary and May will say nothing
And Robert pretends
That he's always been perfectly happy.
Where will it end,
This merry-go-round of evasion,
Part truths and half lies?
I think I'll opt out for the moment
By closing my eyes.

THE GROUP

Mathematics and logic
Cannot account for everything.
We can think of innumerable instances
Where the sum total of
The various parts of a thing
Is not as great as
The sum of the thing itself.

A poem is a good example –
Composed of words
Each having its own meaning
Yet put into context
Gaining in depth and intensity,
So that the poem as a whole
Acquires a power
Beyond the sum of the words.

This group of individuals,
Each dancing to his own tune,
Has imperceptibly begun to merge
So that suddenly we find
Everyone dancing together
Forming a pattern.
Moving but still.
The rhythms tangible
In the silence.

What seems to have happened is,
That after three months
Of very hard work,
We have finally arrived
At the beginning.

MARY

Mary always looked so sad.
Her face was pale, she dressed in black.
She listened from her corner chair
And seemed afraid to say a word.
We missed her when she wasn't there.
Now she's never coming back.

BETH

Devious, blinkered,
Intent on her own desires
The wayward child stokes up
The smouldering fires.

The adult tries to hide
Beneath an accomplished mask
Whose veneered surface takes
The enemy to task.

Passion is controlled
In diplomatic games
But reason cannot quench
The thirsty flames.

Ignored, the shooting sparks
Fade as they alight.
One day a ready fuse
Will ignite.

POWER

Power to the rulers,
The grand and the great,
Premiers and princes,
Ministers of state.
Landowning gentry,
Peers of the realm,
All the proud figures
Who stand at the helm.

Power to the guardians
Defending our shores,
All the officials
Upholding our laws.
Wardens, politicians,
Security chiefs,
Judges and lawyers
Contending their briefs.
Power to the bankers
And business tycoons
Who are paying the piper
And calling the tunes.
Captains of industry,
Union men,
Newspaper magnates
Who rule by the pen.

Power to writers
And singers of songs,
Power to teachers,
Professors and Dons.
Power to doctors
And nurses who care,
Power to the pop stars
And millionaires.
Power to the famous,
The rich and the clever.
But me . . .?
Never.

NICHOLAS

Absence does not necessitate
Increasing fondness of the heart,
But having your absence noticed
Reveals you have a part
In what is happening.
You know you have a place
If your absence
Leaves a space.

THOMAS

Incomprehension threatens, like clouds
Feared over dark impenetrable hedges.
Words tumble words, pursuing each other
Down tortuous paths, their meaning lost
In tangled turnings. Baulked
By a sudden blind alley, the senses jar,
Struggling for balance, distorting reality
Compulsively cowards, lost in a maze
Of misunderstanding, their purpose confused
Their destination uncertain.
How can we make decisions
When thought is incoherent?

MAY

Sitting upright in her chair
With legs together at knees and feet
She clasped her hands upon her lap
Her hair was waved, her clothes were neat.

She listened with a pleasant smile,
And laughed if someone made a joke
But held her silence week by week
Then finally, one day she spoke.

'Last year I took an overdose –
I couldn't stand the mental pain.
Nothing seemed worth living for.
It's likely that I'll try again.'

GILLIAN

These are not my children
But watching the painful struggle
To find their independence
Makes me feel maternal.

These are not my children
But each one is demanding
Sympathy and comfort –
A mother's understanding.

These are not my children
We gather here as equals
To give support and caring
In one another's troubles.

These are not my children
But they need me as a mother,
Assigning me that image,
Denying me another.

These are not my children
I share their infant fears.
If none of them can hear me
Who will dry my tears?

ROBERT

Your name's not Bobby, you were told at school
Here you are Robert, that's our rule.

Losing your name
Was the start of it all.
Trying to avoid
Ridicule
You lost your name
You lost your will
The after-effects
Are with you still.
Suppressing emotions
Hiding your tears
You lost your identity
Over the years.

You learned to conform
And toe the line.
To outward appearance
Everything's fine.
But inside's the anger
And pain and despair
Of the innocent child
Still trapped in there.
For your own sake Bobby.
Rage and shout.
That lost little boy
Is trying to get out.

STEPHEN

No light shines
Beyond the dull grey shadow.
No glow of hope
Defeats the gloom.
The sacrifice of martyrdom
The only satisfaction.
A self-inflicted fate
That suffocates,
Denying choice and freedom –
Like death.

SILENCE

As silence falls across the room

Of quiet thought,

Eye meets eye

And faces smile,

Content to let it lie.

GILLIAN 2

It was a shock
To hear my name
When Tom was talking.
All the same
I felt quite pleased
When out it came.
"Gill said this"
And then again
"When Gill said that".
I don't know why.
I heard a soft
Collective sigh
And glancing round
I caught Beth's eye
Just looking at me –
Steve was too –
As though assessing
Something new.
I couldn't think
What I should do
To stop their gaze.
They didn't smile
Or look away –
So all the while
That Tom was talking,
I kept silent.

FRUSTRATION

I felt
A growing flood of desperation
That everything I said
Was greeted with a knowing smile
Of disbelief.
That twisted mouth
Twisting my words
Towards your own preferred perception.

MARIONETTES

Upon the stage the figures dance,
Perform their play
And work towards an end.
They have their say.

But nothing here is left to chance,
Behind the scenes
The puppet master pulls the strings.
She had the means

To hold them still or make them dance.
You do not see
That when one moves or when one sings
They are not free.

ENVOI

I wanted to write a final poem
To round things off nicely and make them complete,
But I found when I tried that it just didn't work,
The words wouldn't go where I wanted.

Eighteen months is quite a long time
And saying goodbye seemed the right thing to do.
But you can't turn your back on the thoughts in your mind,
Leaving you wasn't an ending.

Though the times that we shared are over and past,
Life doesn't divide into neat little blocks
But experience comes with us as part of ourselves
Whatever it was.

. . . AND NEVER HAVE TO SAY GOODBYE

If time moved backwards

We would know the solution before the problem,

Grow younger every day,

Lose our responsibilities,

And end our lives without regrets.

UNTITLED

This is the secret poem

    that was never written.

It contains all the private thoughts

    I never shared.

These words mark the place

    to remind me.

Blea Tarn

SEASONS

THE GARDEN	*Page* **30**
AUTUMN 1	**31**
AUTUMN 2	**32**
FUTURE IMPERFECT	**33**
SEAGULLS	**34**
SNOWFALL	**35**
SNOWDROPS	**38**
A TASTE OF HEAVEN	**39**

THE GARDEN

Clusters of daisies adorn
The neglected grass. The lawn
Needs cutting. At every corner
Croquet hoops still stand
And mallets lie abandoned
In the rain.
As though everyone left
In the middle of the game.

AUTUMN 1

It's a long time since Spring.
The trees which once were fresh and green
Providing summer's shade
Are now ablaze with gold
In Autumn's glory.
The fading leaves are dying
And soon will gently fall. Between
The stricken branches leaden skies
 Foretell the darker days
Of barren winter, harsh and bleak
As nature dies.
It's a long time 'til Spring.

AUTUMN 2

On longer Autumn days
The air is warm
And golden in the sun
Whose slanting rays
Pierce strongly through the trees
Where, one by one,
The leaves are turning.
Each day has living fire
Each morning new desire.

On shortening Autumn days
The air is chill
Though now the fading sun
Finds myriad ways
To filter through the trees
Where, one by one,
The leaves are fading.
Each night brings winter's breath
Each day a living death.

FUTURE IMPERFECT

The tree's branches are bare
And though a wintry sun
Crawls across the sky
Death is in the air.

The earth yields tangled roots
Upon the barren ground
Leaves return to dust
Beside the withered roots.

The fledgling birds have fled
Now the seeping fogs
Choke the empty nests
Winter lies ahead.

Frost and wind and rain
Pre-empt the coming Spring
And in the twisted limbs
No sap will rise again.

SEAGULLS

Against the dark sky
The swirling shapes
Form a dense cloud,
Floating gently
And drifting lower
Over the field
With eddies and flurries
Till finally
The fugitive gulls
Softly settle.
Foreshadowing the snow
That soon will come.

SNOWFALL

'It's snowing!'. Suddenly I see
The soft white flakes drift gently down.
At first they seem to hesitate
As if unsure of their reception,
Then softly settle on tree and lawn,
Along the fence and on the gate,
And lastly clothe the waiting path
With layers of powdery white.

The snow is getting bolder now.
The heavy flakes fall thick and fast.
A snow cloud fills the sky
And darkness deepens as the night
Draws in. The storm will last
For hours. But in the morning when I wake
I'll see the world transformed in white
Dazzling beneath a clear and bright
Blue sky. A mystic magic world
Of invitation.
                   And yes I know
There may be ice – the treacherous foe
And after that the dirty streets
Play host to insidious slush
That too may trip unwary feet.
And frozen pipes and traffic jams –
And yet . . .
                   And yet
Each time I see the first flake fall
My senses tingle with a magic thrill
Of expectation and delight.
And in my heart
I am a child again.

One Snowy Day

SNOWDROPS

They have no way to count the days
So how is it they know,
Those tiny bulbs beneath the ground
When it's time to grow?

The earth is hard with frost and ice
Yet underneath, unseen,
Striving up towards the light
Are little spikes of green.

And when their namesake melts away
The dainty flowers appear
And snowdrops signal to the world
"Spring will soon be here".

A TASTE OF HEAVEN

Lying back in my garden chair
I watch the clouds go drifting by,
Small puffs of white in clear blue sky.

I'm underneath the whitebeam where
I feel the faintly whispering breeze
That softly stirs the shadowy leaves.

Is it courtship or a fight?
Two blackbirds standing head to head
With chattering beaks and wings outspread.

All of a sudden they both take flight.
From somewhere near a robin sings.
And a bumble bee with buzzing wings

Is busy fumbling summer flowers
To find their nectar – and floating by
I see a white winged butterfly.

I've lain here languidly for hours
Too hot to move – yet all around
I'm entertained with sight and sound.

I ought to stir – but it seems too soon
To end the perfect afternoon.
This lazy, hazy day in June.

The Dark Hedges

IN SOMBRE MOOD

IN THE SHADE	*Page* **42**
I WANTED TO SAY	**43**
TIME RUNS OUT	**45**
IN HOSPITAL	**46**
DECORATING	**47**
ELEVENTH HOUR	**48**
REMEMBERING MIFFY	**50**
APRIL 2020	**51**
NIGHTFALL	**52**
THE CHURCHYARD	**53**

IN THE SHADE

Looking out of my kitchen window,
I see the dark pine
Standing nearby like a sentry on guard.
The tree has a fine
And handsome stature, tall and erect.
I have loved this tree
For many years and watched it grow.
But now I see
It blocks the early morning sun
Which cannot seep
Through the densely laden branches,
And casts a deep
And gloomy shadow. I realise
I have been wrong
To let the tree have its will.
For far too long
I have been living in its shade.
And though I know
It will be hard, the time has come
To let it go –
And I will walk in the sun again.

I WANTED TO SAY

Your parting advice was
"If you care for someone
Be sure that you tell them –
Make certain to tell them
Before it's too late".

I wanted to say
So much –
But there wasn't the time
And I couldn't find words
Before we went
Our separate ways.

I wanted to say
"Go back to the places
You used to enjoy
When your wife was alive".
But inside my head
It sounded too brutal.

I wanted to say
"Visit your grandson
And give him your love,"
But I knew how seeing him
Tore you apart
Because SHE wasn't there.

I wanted to say
"You can cry on my shoulder"
To tell you I knew,
To show you I cared
But I saw from your face
That you valued your pride.

If you had broken down
I would have said
Nothing,
Feeling your pain
And sharing your grief
With my own unshed tears.

TIME RUNS OUT

The shiftless sands of time run out.
What lay ahead
Is now behind,
Its hopes forgotten.
The only certainty is death.

The search for meaning
Is man's prime occupation.
A need for understanding
Leads to religious faith,
Philosophical theory,
Or suicide.

IN HOSPITAL

Death hesitates.
He would be welcome now,
Bringing relief to a siege of milk,
But kindness heads him off.
'Everyone is so kind'.
They are doing their best –
Prolonging a life
That ends like a beginning.

Milk and kindness
Can overcome everything.
They have vanquished proud independence
And the last defences –
Whimpering cries of a second infancy.
With gentle firm insistence
They nourish the body
And kill the spirit.

DECORATING

Three men lie dead on the floor –
A sprawling untidy death.
Their uniforms are crumpled.
They had no time to resist
And one looks surprised
And lolls back in his chair
His open mouth silenced for ever.

Those who used to command
Are now trampled underfoot.
Slowly a white shroud descends
Blotting them out a second time
Leaving here no epitaph.
My job is done.
I pick up my paint pot
And go from the room –
But they lie in eternity.

ELEVENTH HOUR

This is the day we honour the dead
In silence. The red
Of the poppies spatters the crowd
Like the blood that was shed
In the heat of battle. They stand with heads bowed
In the dark dull November
And think of the soldiers, not cowed
By the roar of the guns or the loud
Burst of shells — but instead
Fighting bravely, heroically,
Facing the odds which led
To their deaths, to the peace — to this moment.
The mourners are silent —
Remembering horrors —
The thousands who lost
Their lives or their limbs or their minds,
Knowing the cost
Was too heavy — united in grief
And sense of futility, needing belief
In "never again".

The two minutes pass –

Then with flurry of brass
The military band strikes up a refrain
Stirring the blood and blotting out pain.
The horses are restive, the guards on each back
Are looking quite splendid in scarlet and black.
The troops begin marching – they make a brave sight.
Their training and discipline fit them to fight.
Battalion, platoon and infantry corps
Are ready to follow their leaders to war.
That's what an army is organised for.
So, proud of their potency, heads held up high,
The Generals go by.

REMEMBERING MIFFY

We walked you Miffy, through many long years.
You bounded ahead, sniffing each smell.
We followed behind, sharing laughter and tears.
We never stopped talking, there was so much to tell.

You were lovely and lithe, ever raring to go.
You would bring me a ball with a look that said 'please?'
But if I were ill or sad you would know,
Sitting softly beside me, your head on my knees.

The world has much changed and so have our lives
But the path through the silver birch woods is the same.
The river still flows, the cow parsley thrives
And together we still 'walk the dog' in your name.

APRIL 2020

The fields are looking pretty now.
The blackthorn hedge is white as snow
Along the rim – and at its foot
Cow parsley thrives – a milky row
Of cloudy heads floating gently in the breeze.
And all the grassy slope below
Is carpeted with meadow flowers.
Speedwell, primrose, clover and yarrow
Are scatted here and there,
But buttercups and daisies grow
In gay profusion, side by side
And intermingled. And in amongst them
Golden yellow dandelions show
Their flattened heads – which magically turn
Into those little fluffy balls
That younger children like to blow
To count the hours. And over all
The April sunshine casts its warming glow.

But the people passing to and fro
Do not stop to say Hello,
As once they did some weeks ago,
But pass by at a distance, so
They make no contact, for they know
That danger lies in doing so.

NIGHTFALL

Quiet descends –
The stillness of the after-sun
Whose unseen glow still fringes pink
The dim horizon's roof.
The clear cut sky, a blue infinity
Holds out a guiding hand
And leads my yearning spirit on
Beyond the bounds of earth and space
Through far-off dreams and mystic thoughts
Towards the depths of unknown peace –
Eternity.

But slowly now
The shadowy night comes fingering in
And closes up this mortal world.
The rose has turned to ash
And darkness clouds the crystal sky.
My shrinking soul, in forced retreat
Deprived of that eternal truth
Imprisoned again in earthly doubts
Cries for relief from restlessness
And finds a merciful oblivion
In sleep.

THE CHURCHYARD

From the steeple pointing up to the sun
The morning bell rings bright and clear,
And as the people quickly come
They pass the shaded Churchyard where
A settled congregation waits,
Their places kept by mossy stones.
No heat or light can penetrate
To rouse these ancient Christian bones.
Unseen, unheard and deaf they lie;
But still they touch each passer-by.

Newgale Beach

IDLE THOUGHTS

TO MY FOREBEARS	*Page* 56
THE LOVE SONG OF ANTHEA PRUFROCK	58
BLACK AND WHITE	60
OPTIONS	62
PHILOSOPHICAL POEM	64
VEXATION	65
THE PHYSICAL RAINBOW	66
DISABILITY	67
THIS WASN'T MEANT	68
NEMESIS	69
THE WEATHER FORECAST	70
THE FINAL WORD	71

TO MY FOREBEARS

If the Church is right
And all men have souls
And all are equal in God's sight,
Why then
You too,
Neanderthal man,
Have a soul
Though you
Were dead long before the Church as I know it.

Did you think about God
Neanderthal man
As you hunted the forest and hills for food,
Hunted bears
For skins
And lived in their lairs –
Used stones
And flint to make tools which you buried beside your dead.

Was your God like ours Neanderthal man?
We live in a world of civilised poets,
We eat
From tins
And segregate
Our fellow men
For coloured skins
And could blow ourselves up in a couple of hours.

If the Church makes sense
Neanderthal man,
One day we shall meet in the highest heaven.
Will we care
For each other
And will I have more
In common with you
Than our brother to be born a million years hence?

THE LOVE SONG OF ANTHEA PRUFROCK

You behaved like a bully,
Brushing aside
Our tentative suggestions
With careless contempt.
But when you smiled
I noticed how
The corners of your eyes crinkled.

Your mouth was foul
With "shit" and "sod",
Bloody words,
Grotesque and obscene.
But when you read
A poem aloud
You caressed each word with tenderness.

You were a shambling messy man,
Personal hygiene
Wasn't your forte,
But when you spoke
Your words revealed
A fine and formidable intellect.

Your projected persona
Was macho male,
Assured and arrogant.
Brutalist beast.
But when you dropped
The mask I saw
A maze of doubt and uncertainty.

You taught me nothing
Of literary language.
Our poetic discourse
Didn't meet.
But when the course
Came to an end
I found you'd taught me paradox.

BLACK AND WHITE

White, some say, stands for purity,
Worn by brides.
White lilies on the altar
At Eastertide.
White are the doves of peace
And white is cleanliness,
Detergent weighting –
Next to God.

Black some say is the colour of sin,
Satan's power.
Black are the terrors of night
Evil's magic power
Black is the torturer's pitch,
The wayward sheep
And black the dirt we tread
Beneath our feet.

So is black wrong
While white is right?

White is the falling snow
That sweeps in drifts
And avalanches engulfing men
And freezing them to death.
It turns to messy slush
That hardens into ice
Which maims and kills
Remorselessly.

So white's not always right.

Black to the heart is coal
That burns with cheerful flame
To cast life-giving warmth
And comfort.
Its glowing embers in the furnace
Create the power of steam
And disseminates itself
Into a thousand uses.

Black gives us warmth and light.

So white and black
Are both alright
And things go well
When they unite.
I set this down
In black and white.

Sculpture

OPTIONS

At one time it used to be maidens
Imprisoned in ivory towers.
Now it's top executives,
The admin men and management team,
Confined in self-contained cells
In high-rise office blocks,
Condemned to spend their working lives
With bare necessities –
White desks and telephones
Soft carpeting to dull the noise,
While double glazing shields them
From distant views
Unseen, unreal.

Here inside is what matters.
Here inside are problems pondered,
Meetings attended,
Reports written,
Policies made,
And momentous decisions taken
Affecting the future.
Here inside is the power
That makes the world go round,
The real world,
Their world.

Outside, unnoticed,
The sun shines unbidden,
Birds sing uninvited,
Daisies spring in countless lawns
And children grow.

Outside,
People go about their daily lives
And make a thousand tiny decisions,
Each one seemingly unimportant,
Each one as trivial as a grain of sand,
Together forming solid rock
On which a life is built -
A life in which to bring up children,
Without whom
There would be no future.

PHILOSOPHICAL POEM

In the mid-distance of a summer evening,
Where the brown path curves along the field
And the green grass drifts in a gentle breeze,
Leafy trees form a screen,
And the small boys on eager bikes
Appear and disappear
In careless freedom,
Mysterious in the hazy silence.

All this is only sense data,
Fed to a brain by electrical impulses.
There is no certainty of its existence.
All that can be said for certain
Is that someone, somewhere,
Feels at peace.

VEXATION

Where there is life there is always doubt.
If I do things this way will it work out
For the best? It's hard to say,
Perhaps I could try a different way.
There is always room for improvement I know
And I am not perfect – even so
I sometimes wish you would understand
That when for months I have schemed and planned
And thought about every single thing
To make an occasion go with a swing,
It drives me crazy when on the day
You ARGUE with every word I say.

THE PHYSICAL RAINBOW

According to the Physics laws
For each event there is a cause.
For instance quite a simple action
Can result in light refraction.
Take a light and let it pass
Through a solid block of glass.
The light will bend as it goes through
And split to shades of every hue,
The rainbow colours that we know
From red right through to indigo.
That is how and that is why
You see a rainbow in the sky.
For sometimes in this English weather
The rain and sun will come together.
The sunbeam shining through the rain
Divides into its parts again.
And thus we see the heavenly bow
Its shimmering colours all aglow.
Who would have thought that bending light
Could lead to such a glorious sight.
It lifts my heart and makes me smile
But only lasts a little while.
I know the science. I don't care.
I just enjoy it while it's there.

DISABILITY

The Doctors say I'm visually impaired.
I don't agree.
There are so many things I'm unable to do
Now I can't see.

I can't ride a bike or drive my car
Or read a book.
Sewing's become impossible
And it's hard to cook.

Out in the garden I can't tell a weed
From a valued plant.
It used to be easy to spot the difference.
Now I can't.

I can't play tennis or badminton –
I wish I could.
My skill with Scrabble's a thing of the past
And Sudoku's no good.

Shopping for clothes used to be fun –
Not any more.
When you can't see the colour, the size or the price
It's simply a bore.

The Doctors say I have an 'impairment' –
I don't agree.
With so many things I'm not able to do
It's a DISABILITY!

THIS WASN'T MEANT

This wasn't meant to happen to me,
The aching limbs, the dodgy knee,
The wrinkled face, the wispy hair,
The dizzy spell if I stand on a chair.

This wasn't meant to happen to me,
Frequent visits to my GP,
Hospital trips for various ills
And having to swallow innumerable pills.

This wasn't meant to happen to me,
Fearing the loss of memory,
Ears going deaf, fading sight,
The need to get up several times in the night.

Growing old is clearly no joke
But I thought it was meant for other folk.
I just didn't understand, you see,
That one day all this could happen to me.
I planned to grow old with charm and grace
And perhaps a few laughter lines on my face.

NEMESIS

Oh what folly, to think that we
Are masters of the earth –
So proud of our achievements,
So certain of our worth.
We think we are the pinnacle
Of nature's evolution,
Equipped to solve her problems,
Like the evil of pollution,
And the curse of rising temperatures
And hold with some conviction
That we are duty-bound to save
All creatures from extinction.
We circumnavigate our globe
And work goes on apace
To send man far beyond the moon
And on to outer space
To span new worlds – we were so sure
Of our invincibility.
And then a virus came along
To teach us some humility.

THE WEATHER FORECAST

"If you haven't been out this morning,
It's raining" Carol said.
Well I'm still in my pyjamas
And drinking tea in bed.

But is it really my fault?
Should I take the blame?
I'm sure if I were now outside
The weather would be the same.

And I'm looking out of the window,
My eyes are open wide,
So I don't need someone to tell me
That it's pouring with rain outside.

"If you haven't been out this morning,
It's freezing" Carol said.
Now that's really cool information –
I think I'll have breakfast in bed.

THE FINAL WORD

She planned to have the final word
But someone butted in
And said her views were quite absurd,
Her argument was thin.
Provoked by this there came a third
Entrant to the fray,
Who disagreed with what he'd heard,
And meant to have his say.
By his remarks two more were stirred
And they went head to head
For one agreed and one demurred
With what had just been said.
Then suddenly there came a herd
Of voices in a throng
To state which viewpoint they preferred
And prove the other wrong.
All spoke at once, yet undeterred
They raised their voices higher
And carried on quite unperturbed –
In truth the noise was dire.
The scene was getting murderous
It sounded like a riot –
Till one stentorian voice was heard
"EVERYONE BE QUIET!"

And that's how it occurred
That "quiet" was the final word.

Treeline

FAMILY

TO MY CHILD BEFORE BIRTH	*Page* **74**
MUTUAL DELIGHT	**75**
PIECES OF ART	**76**
THE SCHOOL	**78**
THE HARDEST PART	**79**
TO MY UNKNOWN GRANDCHILD	**80**
THIEPVAL	**81**
CLEAR VISION	**82**
THE FAMILY PHOTOGRAPH	**83**

TO MY CHILD BEFORE BIRTH

You do not know
What is going to happen.
Safe in the sheltering womb
You test your puny limbs
With growing confidence
Against my unresisting abdomen.

You do not know
What is going to happen.
How the unfriendly womb
Will rudely thrust you out
On hard and bony journey
Into an alien world.

You do not know
What is going to happen.
You do not know yet
Of hunger, thirst and cold
Of fear and pain
And newborn loneliness.
You do not know anything.

And I who know
And have prepared,
Cannot prevent that bitter time,
The crowning moment, when
I think you will know fear
And spend your first weak breath
In startled cry.

At that first wakening
You cannot know
How soon my longing arms
Will teach you love.

MUTUAL DELIGHT

Mutual delight
Flows between these two.
Within the shawl, all pink and white.
Pale blue eyes of innocence
Are gazing up at deeper blue
Of wisdom and experience.

Within my heart
There is no pain,
Although it seems I have no part
As they still gaze at one another.
But I am the link that binds the chain.
A daughter and a mother.

PIECES OF ART

Treasure may lie buried
In this jungle room
Where rampant and malignant
Vegetation looms.
Behind the pseudo Triffids
Wherever eye can see
Lurk monsters of creation,
Gems of artistry.

Paintings, drawings, sketches
Are stacked by wall and door,
While miscellaneous flotsam
Drifts across the floor.
All things bright and beautiful,
Banal, begrimed, bizarre,
Are gathered in abundance
A cornucopia . . .

Of sculptures and constructions,
Objects made with string,
Old tin cans and cardboard
And weapons without springs.
Collages and cutouts
Boxes filled with grass
Rubber ducks and pebbles
And fading photographs.

These pearls in precious settings
Are they junk or jewels,
Creative inspiration
Or fantasies of fools?
This pirates' hoard is waiting
The verdict of the years,
The dross will surely tarnish
Gold is what endures.

THE SCHOOL

I passed by the school this morning.
Your old school. By the gate
A boy was standing where you used to wait
For me to pick you up. He wore
The familiar uniform.
It felt so strange to realise
That it isn't your school any more.
Perhaps some influence will remain
But you have cast off the links that bound you
And left them behind.
You are doing the same to me.

THE HARDEST PART

When first I held you in my arms,
My tiny new-born son,
The hard and bitter labour pains
Of giving birth were done.

When first I held you in my arms
The harder task began,
To guide you safely through the years
And raise you to a man.

When first I held you in my arms
How was I to know
The hardest part lay years ahead,
To open wide my loving arms . . .
And let you go.

TO MY UNKNOWN GRANDCHILD

Child of my child, who has no name,
How shall I grieve for you.
You were not born into this world —
You never became
A person we could hold or touch or kiss.
I never saw your smile or heard your cry.

It makes no sense to mourn —
They say you cannot miss
What you have never known —
So someone tell me why
The tears are running down
My face,
        like
                this.

THIEPVAL

Here, where your name is carved
With many thousand others,
Life and time stand still
While homage pays its due.

Here the scant remains
Of fathers, sons and lovers
Are marked by stark white stones
In strictly ordered rows.

Here the silent dead
Unknown but not forgotten
Reach out across the years
And touch the living.

Here I place a photograph
Of one I never knew,
To show I came –
And found your name.

CLEAR VISION

"Long time no see" you said.
But actually
I don't see you. Your face
Is just a blur unless
I scan it from the side.

I don't think that I ever
Saw you properly.
In my rosy tinted view
I thought that you loved me
As much as I loved you.
So I didn't see it coming
And I struggled to believe you
When you said that you were leaving
After all those years.
But now that time has passed
I realise
How often you deceived me –
All those lies.

I never saw right
Through them then
But though my eyes are clouded now
My vision is quite clear
And I see you as you are
At last.
So I'm looking at you
Sideways.

THE FAMILY PHOTOGRAPH

One, two, three, four, five, six Maycrafts are we
All full of frolic and all full of glee.
George E. Maycraft

It is a sunny afternoon
In August. The family,
Whose ages span some eighty years,
Are gathered in the garden
Beside the apple tree,
Some sitting, others standing.
Someone has made them laugh
And all are smiling at the camera
For the family photograph.

Nine of the family were not here,
They lived too far away
To come from Sweden and Australia
And from the USA.
But I'm thinking about my Father
As I view this happy crowd.
He always loved a party
And wrote the Maycraft song
To entertain our relatives
One Christmas time. He was proud
Of his four children
And I wish that he could see,
That twenty-three of the Maycraft clan
Were here on my Eightieth birthday
To celebrate with me.

New Barn

AND FINALLY . . .

THE RED KITE

I saw him sitting on my roof,
Alert and waiting patiently,
Black body outlined
Against the clear blue sky.

Slowly he took off
And for a little while
Circled overhead,
Huge wings outstretched.
I heard his mewling cry
And felt his giant shadow
Passing over me.

Once more he settled on my roof,
Alert and waiting patiently.
The moments slowly passed.
Suddenly he swooped
Out of sight –
And didn't come back.

Footsteps